ETHEREUM

How to Make 36 Times
Your Money in 1 Year

Gary Bukowski

OTHER TITLES BY THE AUTHOR

Blockchain: A 60 minute guide to Blockchain Technology

Bitcoin: How it went from $1 to $2800 in less than 6 years

Table of Contents

Other titles by the Author

Blockchain: A 60 minute guide to Blockchain
Technology

Bitcoin: How it went from $1 to $2800 in less
than 6 years

Introduction

Hello there. Thank you for purchasing this book. 'Ethereum – How to make 36 times your money in 1 year.'

All the information that you will need about Ethereum has been provided in this book in a precise manner. This book has been targeted toward all those people who are curious about investing and trade as well as those who would like to learn about new avenues for earning an income.

The book starts out by giving you a brief understanding of what Ethereum is all about, its founders, the benefits of investing in Ethereum, the process of getting started with Ethereum and the growth potential of Ethereum. This will give you an idea about the rise of Ethereum and why it is an excellent investment opportunity. By the end of this book, you will be equipped with all the information you need for making an informed decision.

So, why don't we get started?

Chapter 1

Brief History of Ethereum

A developer can make use of Ethereum for running Dapps (distributed applications), and this is a peer-to-peer network. These computer programs can be made up of anything, and the network has been optimized to carry out rules that apply in the instance of execution of mechanical standards when a couple of conditions have been met, like a contract for instance. Ethereum makes use of its very own decentralized public blockchain mechanism for storing data in a cryptographical manner, executes it, and even protects these contracts. Every computer on this network will download a very small virtual machine that is made use of for syncing this to the Ethereum blockchain and is available for the execution of different contracts. This diverse network of different computers provides convenience, security, reliability and the computing prowess that you will need for the implementation of particular arrangements.

This network isn't free or even private, so developers just make use of it for obtaining consensus on outcomes and when their data is publicly available. Does that sound technical and complicated? You needn't worry; even I was a little skeptical about Ethereum initially. Only when I got a proper understanding of what this was about could I appreciate Ethereum. Let us take a brief look at the history and development of Ethereum.

In the year 2008, there was a young developer - or rather a developer group - that was responsible for the development of Bitcoin as a novel way for sending value via the Internet. After four years, there was a nineteen-year old who had a dream of creating a new platform that was based on this invention with the aim of transforming the Internet completely. 2011 was the year when Vitalik Biterin, a young programmer from Toronto got interested in Bitcoin. You might or might not be aware of what Bitcoin is. Do you know what CryptoCurrency is? You needn't worry if you don't have an in-depth awareness on this topic. Read on to get a better understanding of this subject.

The Internet was an alien concept a few decades ago. However, the human race would be back in the dark ages without the Internet. The global change in the world of commerce promises to revolutionize the entire political and economic order. Cryptocurrencies lie at the heart of this change. Since the Bitcoin was invented in 2008, the term "CryptoCurrency" has entered our lives. This technology is here to stay, and it will simply keep getting better. CryptoCurrency is relatively cheap, fast, safe and easier to handle as compared to traditional currency and credit cards.

The technology that will have the greatest impact on the world economy and its future is Blockchain technology. Yes, you read it correctly. It isn't solar energy, artificial intelligence or a self-driving car. The initial wave of the digital revolution got us the Internet full of information. The second wave is bringing us block chain technology. This is the age of making use of the Internet for creating more value. It can transform the manner in which business is conducted and the order of human affairs as well. This ingenious protocol allows transactions to be not only anonymous but secure as well. Blockchain is the technology that powers Bitcoin and several other digital currencies. CryptoCurrency is a digital medium of exchange, unlike paper money. It was the first of its kind, and is perhaps the only form of global currency that is free from any intervention by government or regulations.

The value of money isn't determined randomly. It has been assigned a value by the governments of the world. Most of this value is based on the US dollar, and the present global standard helps in determining the value of all the other currencies. The USD is considered to be strong since the United States is presumed to be the strongest economy in the world. This is the reason why its money is influenced by different global perceptions regarding the states and their current events like wars, the balance of trade, credit balance, the reputation of its president, policies, taxes, laws, spending, etc. The USD, the so called global currency standard, has more to do with the way it is perceived rather than the commodities that are responsible for driving it.

Bitcoin represents the hope that one day we will be able to take back what was taken from us way back in the 70s - the Gold Standard. This is a fiat currency but it a peer-to-peer monetary system. You will be in control of how much it is worth. You might be wondering if it would be silly to purchase or make use of Bitcoins that don't have any value. Bitcoins, when they started out in the year 2013, were valued at around $13 per coin. They are assessed at about $550 per coin today. In November 2013, these coins were valued at $1200! The rate of these coins is quite volatile. There is a fixed cap on the number of coins that are available. Therefore, there is only a small chance that inflation would destroy this value.

Now that you know about CryptoCurrency and Bitcoin, we can go ahead and get a better understanding of Ethereum. Vitalik Buterin was the co-founder of Bitcoin Magazine, an online news website and this website was launched in the year 2011. He wrote a lot of articles explaining what CryptoCurrency was. After this, he moved on to code for Dark wallet and Egora. While doing so, he got the idea of creating an ingenious platform that will go well beyond the financial uses that Bitcoin offered. In the year 2013, he released a white paper that gave a description of an idea for an alternative platform that was designed for the different types of decentralized applications that developers could develop. And this system was named as Ethereum.

Ethereum makes it easy for creating smart contracts and self-enforcing code that the developers can make use of for tapping into a variety of applications. Buterin was named as the Thiel Fellow in the year 2014, for the work that he had done it in this field. This contest awards its winners $100,000. Once Buterin had published his white paper on Ethereum, several other developers took to it. The co-founder of Ethereum, Dr. Gavin Wood, had written the yellow paper on Ethereum. This can be thought of as the "technical bible" that gives a detailed outline regarding the specifications of the EVM (Ethereum Virtual Machine) that is responsible for handling the ledger and the operation of smart contracts. Joseph Lubin was the other co-founder of Ethereum, and he founded ConsenSys, a Brooklyn based startup that focused on the creation of decentralized applications.

Buterin, along with the other co-founders of Ethereum, launched a crowdfunding campaign in the year 2014 for getting this project up and running. All the participants in this campaign purchased Ether (also known as Ethereum tokens) that are similar to shares. They managed to raise over $18 million and were considered to be amongst the most successful crowdfunding campaigns ever launched. Proceeds from the Ethereum's initial crowdfunding campaign, as well as the project development, are now being managed by a non-profit entity based in Switzerland known as the Ethereum Foundation.

Chapter 2

Ethereum- The New CryptoCurrency On The Block

The first CryptoCurrency every created was Bitcoin. It was only when Bitcoin became a success that the idea of establishing other crypto currencies came up. Let me tell you a little about Bitcoin. Bitcoin is a type of digital currency; it is created and held in an electronic form. No one has any control over this. Unlike paper currency, these Bitcoins aren't printed, and they are produced by people and different businesses that have electronic operations around the world, making use of software that helps in solving mathematical problems. This is the first instance of the upcoming category of money that is referred to as CryptoCurrency.

Bitcoin can be made use of for buying things electronically. In this sense, they are quite similar to the traditional fiat currencies like the dollar, or euro that are digitally traded as well. The most important characteristic of the Bitcoin and the one thing that makes it different from regular money is that it is decentralized. No single institution is capable of controlling the network of Bitcoins. This will appeal to some people since a large bank isn't controlling their money.

The main aim of Ethereum is to function as a decentralized Internet and also as a decentralized app store that will provide support for the Dapps in this process. No one owns Ethereum; however, the network that supports this is not free. In fact, this network makes use of "Ether." Ether is a specific code that is made use of for paying the computational resources that are necessary for running an application or a program.

Ether is similar to Bitcoin, and it is a bearer asset (quite similar to security in the market, like a bond or a share that is issued in physical form). Ether doesn't require a third party for processing or even approving a transaction, just like cash. It doesn't operate the way a digital currency or payment system would and instead it aims to provide "fuel" that will help in the functioning of the Dapps or decentralized applications on the network. This might sound a little complicated, but it isn't. Think of this as a decentralized online notebook and for deleting, posting or modifying a note. You will be required to pay a transaction fee in the form of Ether to make the necessary changes. Therefore, Ether has also been referred to as digital oil.

If I take this analogy a little further, then the transaction fees on Ethereum are calculated by the amount of gas that is necessary for the action. The transactional cost will depend on the computational power that is required and the time that it would take for getting it up and running. A transaction that would cost 500 gas would be paid in Ether. Thinking of Ethereum from the perspective of an economic system, this is quite open ended. For instance, there is a cap on the number of Bitcoins at 21 million, whereas there is no such cap on the limit of Ether.

In the year 2014, out of all the Ether that is in existence, about 60 million was purchased by the users who participated in the crowdfunding campaign. About 12 million of Ether was directed towards the Ethereum Foundation that consists of researchers and developers who are working on the underlying technology responsible for this. Every 12 seconds or so, there are about 5 Ethers that are allocated to different miners who help in verifying the transactions that take place on the network. In a given year, a maximum of 18 million Ethers can be mined, and about 5 Ether are created in every 12 seconds. This happens whenever a miner happens to discover a block or a bundle of transactions on the network.

The popularity of cryptocurrencies surged once again after the price of Ether had risen to over $400. That's a 5000% increase in its value. The wealth that is produced by this ever-expanding industry is difficult to comprehend, especially when it is difficult to see where the value of this currency is originating. In this section, let us take a look at a deeper look into what Ethereum is all about and how it fares in comparison to Bitcoin.

Ethereum most certainly did not appear out of thin air, regardless of what its name might suggest. It makes use of the similar blockchain technology that Bitcoin uses. However, its platform is Turing-complete, and this is the reason why it is also referred to as programmable blockchain. This would imply the scope for the development of better functionality and advanced applications, including other cryptocurrencies as well, while, on the other hand, Bitcoin just has one function. It is a type of digital currency that helps in peer-to-peer transactions. The first CryptoCurrency that made use of the blockchain technology was Bitcoin. The limited function and scope that it has to offer have created scaling issues for Bitcoin.

The important features of the Ethereum blockchain network are smart contracts and Ethereum Virtual Machine. These features are the reason why Ethereum network is so much more than just a regular system of payment that makes use of digital currency. Contracts that are written in code and are considered to be self-executing are known as Smart Contracts.

An example will help you in getting a better understanding of this concept. For instance, let us look at a situation where I have made a bet of $100 with Tom that Ether will be valued at $600 USD at the end of this month. Once I have agreed to the terms and conditions, Tom and I draw up a Smart Contract. This Smart Contract is now available on a public ledger and therefore it can neither be tampered with nor any adjustment can be made to the same without breaking down the underlying code that this program is made up of. Now, let us assume that, by the end of this month, the value of Ethereum is still under $600 USD. If this had been a regular contract or even an oral agreement, then I have the option of saying something like "I was just kidding," "I wasn't serious," or even something like "I don't have the money." If Tom wants to get his $100, then he will have to drag me to court to get the contract executed in his favor. Well, with a Smart Contract, I can bypass the shortcomings of an ordinary contract. This means that the terms on which the deal has been formed are programmed before execution and are programmed according to the terms that have been agreed upon.

Other blockchain technologies are capable of executing a Smart Contract, Ethereum has this feature embedded into his payment system, it allows for immediate transfer of value across the global market this is decentralized with zero-downtime, and there are no middlemen involved in this process.

The Bitcoin was created with the intention of being used for the transfer of monetary value. According to the creators of Ethereum, it merely acts as the "gas or fuel" for Smart Contracts. Ethereum can be made use of as a tool of accumulation and transmission of value (it does this with faster transactions than the ones that are offered by the blockchain network of Bitcoins). However, initially, the ETH was intended not just for this but also for providing some functionality to the Smart Contracts (the contract initiators will need to spend some amount in the form of Ether for this purpose, and it can be compared to the transaction fees or the commission charge that banks levy while facilitating a contract). These fuels aren't supposed to be expensive, and the same stands true for Ethereum or Ether as well.

With an increase in the price of Ethereum, the functioning of these smart contracts becomes involved; this is caused due to the increase in the expenses of the execution of the code. This is the reason why the use of ETH as an artificial asset and the exaggeration of price rates, that tend to take place on the exchanges for CryptoCurrency can harm the essential functions of Ethereum and affect its reliability as well.

Coming back to the real world, ETH transactions have gradually slowed down since the Initial Coin Offering (ICO), this has gained its name from the resemblance it shares with IPO (Initial Public Offering) conducted by a company. In an ICO, the companies will offer their tokens or coins that have been created on the Ethereum platform, as an option for obtaining the necessary investments for funding the development of technologies. When there is a high level of interest that has been shown for an ICO, and there are too many people who are interested in buying Ether, then in such a case, the network has shown certain limits. However, the group of developers and programmers at Ethereum are working on fixing these scalability issues.

The Ethereum Virtual Machine, also referred to as EVM, is a universal computer. The EVM provides its developers the ability not just to operate but even execute almost any kind of application over this network. The EVM facilitates in decentralizing the program operations in a transparent and fully secure network of blockchain technology. If that sounds slightly confusing, then let me explain it further. Think of the Internet as a series of nodes that are connected in the structure of the web. In a situation like this, a server would be the central node that would provide connectivity to several other smaller nodes (like your desktop or PC).

In a topology like this, if there is an attack, then large portions of the Internet can be taken out as happened in the Amazon AWS outage. The decentralization and the distribution of information in the form of identical blocks that are secured cryptographically across the whole network help Ethereum in getting rid of all the vulnerable points that most of the servers forming the backbone of the Internet suffer from.

GPU mining has made a comeback as well. A regular user will not be able to take advantage of their GPUs for mining Bitcoins since this process has become extremely intensive. These days, mining is being controlled by companies based in China, where the cost of electricity is way cheaper than it would be in the United States.

Well, you might have noticed that the AMD Radeon Rx-series cards aren't easily available, or they are available for exorbitant prices. It seems like they are just sold out. Well, they are, and these graphic cards are in high demand for satisfying the needs of amateur as well as professional miners. A mining rig that is considered to be useful would consist of a motherboard, an entry-level processor, and about five to ten GPUs. You can build your rig for around $2500. However, they are being sold for over $3000 per rig. This goes to show that there is a high demand for GPUs in the market and it cannot be satisfied especially when the value of Ether is increasing rapidly. GPU mining is being considered to be profitable once again. Despite the shortage of AMD cards, you can still stay in the game by making use of Nvidia GPUs that are capable of computing blockchain hashes quite efficiently.

Like me, you may also be wondering how GPUs can be made use of for mining Ether effectively but not Bitcoin. Well, the answer lies in the consensus algorithm that has been designed for Ethereum. The network that Ethereum makes use of has an algorithm that is referred to as Ethash. Ethash is ASIC resistant, and it is PoW (proof of work) algorithm. To simply state things the miners will be entitled to receiving blockchain rewards or Ether because of Ethash by computing a few transactions that have been selected randomly.

According to the whitepaper on Ethereum, this design has two outcomes. The first one is that the Ethereum contracts can use any form of computation, so the ASIC of Ethereum would be an ASIC for general computation that is it will be a better CPU. The second outcome is that the process of mining would require the miner to access the entire blockchain and this means that they will need to store the entire block chain to verify the transactions that take place. This means that it is not necessary for centralized mining pools.

As I have mentioned earlier, CryptoCurrency Ethereum is also referred to as ETH or Ether, and it was developed in the year 2014. This CryptoCurrency is quite similar to the other kinds of cryptocurrencies that are in existence. Ether makes use of blockchain technology and cryptographic protection as well. Just like the other crypto currencies, even this one can be traded on CryptoCurrency exchanges, or it can even be exchanged for other cryptocurrencies. There are a few features of Ethereum that make it stand out. I have discussed these features in this section.

Founded by Vitalik Buterin

In the year 2013, Vitalik Buterin came up with the idea of creating Ethereum while being an active participant in the Bitcoin community. The first white paper he published on

Ethereum helped in paving the way for creating Ethereum. Along with Dr. Gavin Wood, in the year 2014, he co-founded Ethereum. The formal announcement about Ethereum was made by Buterin in Miami at the North American Bitcoin Conference in 2014, in the month of January. The yellow paper created by Dr. Gavin Wood in April in the same year serves as a technical guide for the same. After this, Ethereum has been integrated into various programming languages like Java and Java script that have improved the performance of the software.

It is available on different platforms

When I started thinking about investing in Ethereum, I wasn't sure about the place where I could acquire Ether. After a little bit of research, I realized that Ether is actively traded on different platforms and it is not restricted to just one platform. Here are a few platforms that offer different ways for trading ETH. If you are skeptical about risking all your hard-earned money, but you still want a share of the action taking place, then there is a platform that will fit the bill. Trading Game helps you in trading in Ethereum without any additional costs, and it is a free application. So, all that you will need to do will be to get started with exploring the features of this application. Poloniex is a trading platform that has recorded the highest trading volume. Poloniex holds a considerable portion of the Ether market, and it offers several currency pairs like ETH/USDT, ETH/BTC, ETC/BTC, and so on. This platform also allows for trading of Ethereum Classic.

Origin of the name "Ethereum"

The founder of Ethereum, Buterin, had come across the name Ethereum while he was browsing through a list of elements listed in science fiction. Vitalik liked the word ether and the meaning associated with it. Ether means air, and it also represents a medium that is permeable to light. If you were interested in playing WoW, then you will have perhaps wondered if he got the idea of the name "Ethereum" from the Ethereal race in the game that resides in Netherstorm. Any link from this game to Ethereum is purely incidental and nothing more than it.

The steady increase in price

The initial price of Ether was established at 200 ETH for every BTC. This implied that one ETH was worth a couple of cents at the most. Things sure did change for Ethereum. The trading price of Ethereum in July 2017 was recorded at $407. This means that there has been an almost 5000% rise in the price of ETH. The second largest CryptoCurrency in the world is Ethereum, and it is right behind Bitcoin that has been valued at $48.9 billion. The current market value of Ethereum is pretty high, and it has huge growth potential. Ethereum and Bitcoin are rivals as you must be aware, and it will be quite interesting to see Ethereum functioning at its full capacity. I don't know about you, but I am fascinated to see if Ethereum will be able to overthrow Bitcoin to become the largest CryptoCurrency base in the world. Analysts are quite sure that the price of Ethereum is bound to increase rather steeply by the end of 2017. One thing that all analysts agree on is that Ethereum has a bright future ahead.

Increase in online search interest

I always feel like gathering a lot of information about something before I make a purchase. This usually means that I open up a search engine and gather the relevant information. During the first quarter of 2017, Ether's search had reached a new high. You might not be aware of it, but there is a relationship that exists between the search interest and the price of ETH in the previous years. Ethereum has indeed come a long way from being something that people weren't aware of to something of great value and purpose. I am glad that Ethereum's popularity is increasing. Did you know that most of the people who have shown interest in Ethereum happen to be from Switzerland?

Relation between Ethereum and banks

Taking into consideration the nature of banking industry and also the high level of security that banks will need for protecting their interest as well as their customer's interest, it can be said that Ethereum can be helpful for banks. The value of Ethereum will keep on increasing as banks start moving towards applications based on blockchain technology that use Smart Contracts for automating the financial process. As the demand for Smart Contracts will increase, the value of Ethereum will increase as well. At present, there are about 11 major banks like Barclays, UBS, HSBC, and many more. These banks have got together with R3 (a startup and an innovation firm that aims at uplifting the role of technology in routine operations) for testing a system. This system will help banks in making use of blockchain for the sake of trading. This test is crucial because it makes use of the blockchain technology that is developed by Ethereum for enabling a Microsoft platform to run on it. If this test turns out to be a success, then not only will it mean that Ethereum will be incorporated into the banking system of these banks, but also revolutionize the entire banking system.

Platform

Frontier was the initial version of Ethereum, and it was a beta release that provided the developers with a platform for experimenting and learning before they can get started with the creation of decentralized apps and tools that were based on Ethereum. On 30th July in the year 2015, Frontier was launched. The next version of Ethereum that was released was known as Homestead, and it was published on 14th March in the year 2016 (on the Pi Day). This was the first ever production release of Ethereum. This upgrade had plenty of changes made to the protocol and the networking change that allowed for further updates in the network. Two more steps are on their way, and their release date hasn't been confirmed yet. The third phase is known as Metropolis and the fourth one as Serenity.

History of Ethereum

Ethereum required a lot of resources before it could take off. There were plans of conducting a pre-sale of the Ether coins or tokens that will allow in amassing sufficient funds for creating different legal entities like the Ethereum Foundation based out in Switzerland. In 2014 in the month of July, a 42-day long public presale of Ether was conducted, and Ethereum had distributed its Ether tokens. The event helped in scoring 31591 Bitcoins that were valued at more than $18 million and at that time the same were exchanged for 60 million Ether. The amount of this exchange was made use of for settling the legal debts and paying the wages to its developers.

It isn't an overnight success

Ether or ETH holds the second largest part of the CryptoCurrency market, right after Bitcoin. During the first quarter of 2017, the market share of Ether has increased by $7 billion, and its price has increased more than five times. When compared to its performance in 2015, the value of ETH has grown more than 2800% since that year. The volume of trade taking place in Ether has been fluctuating, and it will keep on doing so. Ether has got great potential, and this is reflected in its present worth. Ether wasn't an overnight success, it has indeed come a long way since it started and it is bound to go further.

Ether's market

When Ether was created, it wasn't meant to be made use of as a universal digital currency like its rival Bitcoin. The primary function of Ether is to be used as a method of payment for certain actions taking place on the Ethereum network. Ether is supported by the same markets that support the Bitcoin network and Ether can be easily procured from different platforms like Bitfinex and even Kraken. The progression of Ether in the market wasn't as smooth as that of Bitcoin. The growth of Bitcoin was quite gradual, and it took a while for more users to start mining this CryptoCurrency. However, when it comes to Ethereum, it required a presale and donations for procuring the necessary funds for its development. The pre-sale had helped in securing 60 million Ether along with another 12 million Ether that went into the fund for development. So, the first supply of Ether amounted to 72 million with a protocol that states that with every block that is mined 5 ETH would be created. Following this protocol set in place, a maximum of 18 million ETH was permitted to come into play every year after this event. Ethereum is steadily developing; however, it isn't free from criticism. It has been criticized on a couple of security issues, and most of the negativity towards ETH was during the initial stage of development. When compared to Bitcoin, Ethereum is better. However, there is scope for further improvement, and the developers at Ethereum are working on it.

The future of Ethereum does seem quite bright, especially with the rapid increase in the price of Ethereum in this year. All we can do is wait and watch how it grows. The potential of Ethereum is limitless and like everyone else, I am eager to see what Ethereum has in store for its users.

Chapter 3

Should You Invest In Ethereum?

In recent times, the price of Ethereum has increased manifold, and it has outperformed other crypto currencies present in the market. You might be wondering whether you should invest in Ethereum or not and if it is worth investing in.

CryptoCurrency is considered to be an excellent investment because of the following reasons.

Scam

Cryptocurrencies are digital, and they cannot be forged. Not just that, they cannot be reversed arbitrarily by the sender just like the charge backs on the credit card.

Instant settlement

Purchasing real property involves a few third parties (like lawyers or notary), delays, and also the payment of a fee. Bitcoin or CryptoCurrency can be thought of as an extensive database of property rights. Bitcoin contracts can be designed and then enforced to either eliminate or add the approvals of a third party. Any reference to external facts should be completed at a date in future for a fraction of the expense and the time required for the completion of the traditional asset transfer.

Lower fees

No transaction fee is levied on CryptoCurrency exchange since the network already compensates the miners. Even though there is no transaction fee, most would expect that the users would make use of a third party service such as Coinbase for the creation and the maintenance of their Bitcoin wallets. These services are similar to PayPal and provide the online exchange system for Bitcoins and are likely to charge a user fee. PayPal neither accepts nor transfers Bitcoins.

Identity theft

When you give your credit card to a vendor or a merchant, then you will be giving them access to your credit line, regardless of the quantum of the transaction. Credit cards usually operate on what is referred to as pull basis. This means that once the store has initiated the payment, then the assigned amount would be automatically drawn from your concerned account. CryptoCurrency, on the other hand, makes use of a push technique. This would mean that the holder of the CryptoCurrency could send exactly the amount that the owner would want to the merchant.

Access to everyone

There are more than 2.2 billion people out there who have got access to the Internet or even mobile phones but don't have access to the traditional exchange. Such people are the ones that are suited for CryptoCurrency. M-PESA is a mobile-based service that helps in transferring money and also in micro financing. This service has also announced a Bitcoin device, and now one in every three Kenyans has got a Bitcoin wallet.

Decentralization

A huge network of computers all over the world makes use of Blockchain technology for managing the CryptoCurrency database and the transactions. Bitcoin is regulated by a system, and it is not controlled by a single authority. Decentralization in here would signify that the network would operate on a peer-to-peer basis or a user-to-user basis. This helps in forming collaboration instead of a controlling authority.

Universal recognition

Exchange or interest rates don't bind cryptocurrencies; they don't have any transaction fees or any other charges applicable in any country. This makes them suitable for international usage without having to face any problems. This will, in turn, help in saving time and money for conducting business, instead of having to spend hours, for transferring money from one country to another. It can operate at an international level and can be used with ease.

There isn't an electronic cash system that you can make use of wherein your account wouldn't be owned by a third party. For instance, take the example of PayPal. If the company has decided that your account has been or is being misused for any reason, then it has got the power to freeze all of your assets without having to consult you. It is then your responsibility to get it all cleared up for regaining access to your funds. When you use CryptoCurrency, you will have a private key that would have a corresponding public key that would make up the address of your CryptoCurrency. This cannot be taken away from you unless you lose it on your own. CryptoCurrency has got a long road ahead of itself before it is capable of replacing traditional forms of currency and credit cards before being accepted as the global commerce tool.

These were the general advantages that any of the cryptocurrencies would possess. Well, I would like to tell you that Ethereum not only has all the benefits that have been mentioned above but has other added benefits as well. So, read on to learn more about this dynamic CryptoCurrency.

Ethereum was developed by keeping Smart Contracts in mind, and it is more powerful and versatile than the Bitcoin. Here are a few reasons why you should consider treating it as a part of your long-term investment portfolio.

Future investment

Ethereum is among the important platforms of value. There has been a visible shift in the global financial technology industry towards the applications based on blockchain technology for meeting their requirements, execution of Smart Contracts, and the automation of the financial process. Ethereum seems like a tailor-made application for meeting these needs. Regardless of the reason, there has been an increase in the demand for Ether, and this will mean that there will be an increase in the price of Ethereum as well. The fundamental law of demand suggests that there would be an increase in the price of the commodity when there is an increase in its demand and vice versa. Now, let me apply the same law of the request to the Ethereum network. I will be able to infer that with an increase in the demand for not just this platform, but also the ability to execute Smart Contracts, the price of this CryptoCurrency will steadily increase.

Ethereum has got a good scope in the realm of commerce. Ethereum can be successfully made use of in adding value to interbank transactions, any B2B remittance, and other Smart Contracts. The price of Ethereum has certainly experienced lots of appreciation in 2017, and it is bound to increase further given the present conditions. Ethereum hasn't been adopted into the mainstream operations, but there are hundreds or even thousands of applications that are in development stage. More and more people are taking up the task of developing decentralized applications and the parties involved in this work are quite varied (governments, individuals, small business, and even corporations). This, in turn, helps in fueling the demand for Ether, which will lead to an appreciation in its value.

Provides stability

The growth of Ethereum isn't predictable, but it has been quite stable. There haven't been any huge spikes in its value, and its growth is entirely organic. Even with all the cyber-attacks, the demand for Ethereum hasn't decreased. The price of Ether (the CryptoCurrency of Ethereum network) is stable. ETH has made the most of the destabilization and has provided the world with a low-cost alternative option. There are a few investors who have been investing in Ethereum for the growth potential that they see in it, and then there are those investors who just go with the flow. There has been an increase in the demand for this CryptoCurrency and this increase in demand indicates its potential. This has led to an increase in the price of Ether, and it will continue to do so.

At present, there are about 1/3rd as many transactions on the Ethereum blockchain network as on the Bitcoin one. However, the growth rate of Ethereum is exponential while Bitcoin has maxed out its capacity. Cryptocurrencies have a healthy relationship with the force of demand. If there is an increase in the number of people who are using it, the utility and its value will increase as well. Keeping this in mind, I think it is highly unlikely that there would be a reduction in the value of Ethereum as long as its usage shows an upward trend.

Security

There is no point in obtaining money unless you can secure it and fortifying private keys can be quite severe. You can make use of address with multiple signatures, and then put the key in different bank vaults on different continents. Wouldn't this just make it difficult for you to spend your money? You might even have your access key on your phone, but this would just make it difficult to secure your money. Now, let us take a bank account for instance. There is some logic for creating transactions on a monthly basis. That code used will be present on one computer, and it will be executed by the bank. When it comes to Smart Contracts that use blockchain technology, the logic will be running simultaneously on all the nodes (Participating systems or computers), and then the results would be compared with that of the other participants. Members can only change their version of the ledger if they are in agreement with the results. In theory, blockchain is designed in such a way that no one can cheat it.

Ethereum functions as a public blockchain network that is considered to be the most advanced blockchain that is Smart Contract enabled. It has a Turing complete coding system. With this method of coding, you will be able to put any logic into the smart contract allowed by Ethereum, and it will be run on the entire network. Certain mechanisms are in place for preventing the misuse of this network, and you will need to pay for the computing power by giving

"ETH" tokens that will the payment given to the miners for running your code.

To put it simply, Ethereum does stand out amongst all the blockchain technologies present out there.

An excellent team

Vitalik Buterin is a programmer from Toronto, and he grew interested in Bitcoin in the year 2011. He was 17 when he learned about Bitcoin, and in the following year, he won a Bronze medal at one of the International Olympiads in Informatics. He was the co-founder of Bitcoin Magazine, an online news website and wrote a lot about CryptoCurrency. At present, he plays the role of the chief scientist at the Ethereum Foundation (it is a non-profit organization that is based out in Switzerland, and he helps in maintaining the core technology responsible for powering CryptoCurrency). After he had published the white paper on Ethereum, several other developers got on board.

I always like to research about the team behind a project before I make an investment. The team behind Ethereum is smart,

dedicated and quite creative. I feel very
confident about the capabilities of those
behind the functioning of Ethereum.

Chapter 4

How To Buy Ethereum?

I am not sure how you feel, but I certainly regret not buying Bitcoins when they cost a few pennies. At present, they are worth so much more than gold. I kept thinking if I would ever get another chance and well, it looks like I did. Ethereum has given me this opportunity. Investing in Ethereum is a good option, and by doing so, you will be able to reap all the benefits that have been mentioned in the previous chapter. According to market capitalization, Ethereum is the second largest CryptoCurrency that is present, and it is poised overtake Bitcoin as well. The value of the Ethereum tokens has indeed grown at an exponential rate, and it is bound to keep on increasing. Here are a few steps that you will need to take for incorporating Ethereum into your investment portfolio.

Creating an account on the exchange

As with any other crypto currencies, even Ethereum needs to be purchased and sold online via exchanges dealing in this. There are plenty of trading platforms. The most popular options include Kraken, BItstamp, Coinbase, and Gemini. Before you can start trading in Ethereum, you will need to select an exchange and then create an account on it.

Verifying the account

A good exchange will need for you to verify your account in multiple ways. You might be required to upload a couple of documents for verifying your identity and ensuring that your account clears all the necessary regulations. Verification can take a day or two, and it would depend on how popular and busy the exchange that you have opted for actually is.

Depositing fiat currency

The next step would be to deposit fiat currency into the account through your bank or even a wire transfer. This would take a day or two for the money to get clearance.

Start trading

When your account is verified, and money has also been deposited in it, then you can start purchasing or trading in Ether and other cryptocurrencies as well. The interface of each exchange would be different, and you need to have some patience for getting all the necessary clearances and for confirming the transactions.

Withdraw the Ether into a wallet

Once you have purchased ETH on the exchange, the next step would be to withdraw the Ether into a wallet that's under your control. Exchanges are vulnerable to being hacked, and this would mean that your tokens are capable of being stolen. For making sure that your tokens are safe and secure, you will need to store them in a safe place. You will learn more about wallets in the coming chapters. You will need to install a wallet that can handle Ethereum, run and set it up, and create an account for yourself. Once you do this, you can then feed your account address into your account on the exchange, and this will allow you to transfer your Ether into the wallet. Make sure that you don't lose your private key, your wallet, or password. If this happens, then you won't be able to access your Ether later on.

Dealing with volatility

It is quite reasonable for the market to suffer some form of volatility and some markets happen to be more sensitive than others due to a host of reasons. Commodities and currencies are the most volatile of all. The market for crypto currencies is much more volatile than all the other markets. The reason is that the transaction speed, as well as the cost, is as low as it possibly can be. Volatility also depends upon the players in the market. Big players tend to provide some stability to the market, and when they are missing, the market isn't that stable anymore. Dealing with volatility is quite simple. You will just need to get your emotions under control and keep a calm mind so that you can take the right decision.

Flash crash is quite common, and you should anticipate these. This helps in getting rid of any speculation that might exist in the market. Don't focus on the price drop, instead, concentrate on the price level. Acceptance of the market mechanisms is the only manner in which you will be able to deal with a flash crash. You should hold onto Ethereum on a long-term basis. You need to understand that cryptocurrencies have great potential that hasn't been tapped into yet. The upside of holding onto Ether for an extended period is a good option. Don't let one flash crash discourage you from doing so. For instance, look at Bitcoins. They were quite cheap when they were launched, and now they are costlier than gold! Be smart while you are buying Ether. If there is a discount on it, then you should certainly buy it. The price of ether is bound to increase sooner than later, and then you can cash in on the appreciated value of the token.

Chapter 5

How To Use Ethereum?

Does the thought of using Ethereum seem intimidating? Well, even I thought so. However, it isn't all that difficult. If the unstoppable global computer can be developed according to the plan, then it would certainly provide alternatives to all the web applications that are currently quite popular. Ethereum isn't as intuitive as the web that we are used to today, but anyone with a computer or even a smartphone can use this platform as long as they have Ether tokens.

Ethereum wallets

You will need a secure place for storing your Ether or your private keys. This brings me to the concept of Ethereum wallets. There is one important thing that you should be aware of. Losing your private key isn't the same as forgetting your password. You lose your key, and you will lose all the Ether, forever! Getting rid of trusted parties is a double-edged sword. On the one hand, it helps in getting rid of intermediaries and middlemen for verifying transactions and on the flipside; this means that there won't be any help desk to turn to when you lose your private key. Keeping this in mind, there are multiple wallet options to choose from for storing your CryptoCurrency. There could be a desktop, hardware, web, and even paper wallets. Depending upon your preferences or convenience and security you can select any of these options. Usually, convenience and security are at odds with one another. The more convenient something is, the less secure it is and vice versa.

Desktop wallets

These would run on your PC or your laptop. One option available would be to download an Ethereum client. There are a couple of Ethereum customers who have written in different programming languages and different tradeoffs. The entire process can take a few days and will only increase as and when Ethereum grows. The wallet will need to be synced with all the transactions that take place on the blockchain network.

Mobile wallets

Mobile clients are also referred to as light customers, and they will require secondary data that needs to be downloaded to connect to the network and start transacting on it. Such clients can download the wallet on their smart phone. This option is quite convenient but isn't as safe as the previous one. Full Ethereum clients would offer a secure way for receiving transactions since they don't trust the miners or the nodes for sending them proper information- they will validate the deal by themselves. Storing your private keys on the device that is not attached to the Internet is referred to as the cold storage method and is harder to hack. However, this method is best suited for storing large holdings of Ether.

Hardware wallets

These are small and don't take up much space. These wallets provide the best of both wallets mentioned above. These devices are quite secure, and they can be detached from the Internet as well. You can sign transactions without having to be online. However, this isn't a really good option if you are on the move or would like to use your wallet frequently.

Paper wallets

Another cold storage wallet option that you have would to print or even write down the private key on a piece of paper and then lock this up in a safe or a deposit box. Online tools can provide key pairs directly on your system, and this could make your keys vulnerable if the site gets hacked. You can also generate keys by making use of the command line, provide you have got the required cryptographic packages that have been installed in the preferred language. As I mentioned earlier, please be careful with your private keys. If you lose it, then there is no way in which you can retrieve it once again. If it is gone, then it is gone for good. So, I would suggest that you take a few alert messages and create multiple copies of the core and stash them in different secure spots.

Purchasing Ether

Purchasing Ether would vary according to the currency used. You will need to find someone either on the Internet or even in a person who has got Ether and would want to trade it. The option of meeting in person for buying and selling Ether is a viable one if you happen to live in a city where Ethereum meetups are organized, like New York or even Toronto. This might not be an option if you are residing in a less populated area. Some exchanges would allow the users to buy Ether with dollars or even Bitcoin directly. These exchanges usually have a sign-up process. However, if you want to buy ether with another currency would require an additional step. The most popular CryptoCurrency that is used for trading is Bitcoin. Once you have managed to secure some Ether, you can directly send it to another person. There would be a transaction fee that will need to be paid to the miners.

If you are familiar with Bitcoin, then you might have noticed that the way the wallets and the exchange function are quite similar to Bitcoin. However, the Ethereum applications are different. Users who have Ether can join or even create their Smart Contracts (code that will automatically execute the terms of a contract without the involvement of a third party). Bundles of these Smart Contracts can be combined for creating Dapps. However, before we move on from this topic, let us take a look at how it works. Ethereum and various other crypto currencies tend to have a storage system that is quite confusing. Did you ever notice the string of numbers on your credit card? This is necessary for the banks for determining where the money should be sent when the card has been swiped. Well, cryptocurrencies also allow you to generate a set of identification numbers that are quite similar when funds need to be debited. In this sort of system, there are two things that the user would need for the sake of identification. The first one is a public key, and the next one is a private key. These keys are usually displayed as a string of numbers and letters; then these two keys will be put together through cryptography.

The public key can also be sent to others so that they will know where the funds need to be addressed. If you want others to send you Ether, then you will need to give them an address. This would be a scrambled string consisting of letters and numbers that are derived from a scrambled up public key so that people would know where to send the coins. For spending Ether, you will need to sign the funds with a private key. A private key, as the name implies is quite similar to a password. Getting back to the credit card analogy, the private key is akin to the pin that you will need for unlocking your funds for processing a transaction.

One advantage of having an open blockchain system is that the users will be able to generate an identification number for their funds at any given point of time. You don't have to wait for the approval of the bank for processing the transaction, and you needn't present the credit card as well.

Chapter 6

Ethereum Mining

Miners have an important role to play in making sure that Ethereum works. This role isn't an obvious one. Most of the new users tend to think that the only purpose of mining is for generating Ethers in a manner that doesn't need a central issuer. They aren't wrong in thinking so. The Ether tokens are created through a process of mining that helps in creating 5 Ether tokens per block that are mined. However, mining has got another important role that it plays. It is a usual practice for banks to keep an accurate record of the transactions taking place. They help in making sure that the money isn't being created out of thin air, and that the users aren't cheating and spending the money they earned more than once. Blockchain's have helped in introducing an entirely different method of maintaining networks.

In this, the entire network, instead of just an intermediary will assist in the verification of transactions, and it will keep on adding them to a ledger that is public. The goal of a blockchain technology is to create a monetary system that helps in improving the trust of all those who use it; there needs to be someone who will assist in securing all the financial records and for making sure that no one is using any unfair means to cheat. One innovation that helps in making this system of decentralized record keeping a reality is mining.

Miners will be able to come to a consensus about a particular transaction and at the same time prevent fraud as well (prevent double spending of the Ether tokens). This is quite an interesting problem that couldn't be solved in the decentralized form of currencies before the invention of Proof of Work (PoW) blockchain technology. The developers at Ethereum are trying to look into alternative methods reaching consensus regarding the validity of a transaction. Till then, mining will help in keeping this network together.

The mining process that is employed by Ethereum is quite similar to the one that Bitcoin uses. For every block of the transaction, the miners will need to use their hardware or computers for quickly guessing answers to the puzzles until one of them is the winner. If I have to be more specific, then the miners will have to run the unique Meta data of the header through a series of hash functions (that will give out a fixed length of scrambled numbers and letters that seem random). Only the "nonce" value will change, and this would impact the hash value thus created. If the miner happens to find a hash that is a match to the given target, then the miner will be able to get his hands on the Ether and also broadcast this block on the network for getting the validation of different nodes and adding their copy of this to the ledger. If miner A happens to find the hash, then miner will B will stop working on the current block and then start the same process all over again for the next block that comes up.

It is quite difficult for miners to cheat here and there is no possible way in which this work can be faked and obtain the correct answer to this puzzle. This method of solving the puzzle is referred to as "proof of work" or PoW for the sake of convenience. It hardly takes any time for the other nodes for verifying whether the obtained hash value is right or not. A miner finds a block on the Ethereum network every 12-15 seconds. If the miner starts to solve the puzzles quicker or slower than this, then the algorithm will adjust the difficulty of the miner so that the miners get around 12 seconds for solving the puzzle. The miners can earn Ether tokens randomly. However, their profitability certainly depends on their luck and also the amount of computing power that had to be devoted to this.

The PoW algorithm that Ethereum network makes use of is referred to as Ethash. This has been designed in such a manner that it requires a lot of memory to make it tougher to mine using ASICs (these are individual chips that are the only profitable way in which Bitcoins can be mined) that are expensive. Ethereum has got plans of shifting from PoW algorithm to PoS algorithm. Therefore, I would suggest that you don't stock up on ASIC since they might not prove to be of any use in the long run.

Ethereum might not need miners forever. The developers of Ethereum are planning on replacing the proof of work algorithm (the algorithm the Ethereum network makes use of for validating a transaction and also for preventing any cheating) with a Proof of Stake (PoS) algorithm where the network will be secured by the owners of the Ether tokens.

Chapter 7

How Can Ethereum Be Mined?

Now that you know what Ethereum mining is and how it works, like me, even you will want to know how you can extract Ether on your own. Let me give you a quick recap of the previous chapter. Mining can be thought of as the glue that is responsible for holding the decentralized application store of Ethereum together by making sure that it comes to a consensus on every change made to its Dapps that are running on the network. Think of the blockchain network as an online notebook and network will not be able to come to a consensus about the said state of the notebook (when a note is added, deleted or any modification has been made to it) without the computational prowess that is necessary for processing these changes. So, miners will need to make use of their computers for solving any cryptographic puzzles in their bid to win Ether. They will need to try a lot of computational problems until they find one that will help in unlocking a new block of the asset.

One fascinating aspect about an open blockchain is that anyone will be able to set their computers for focusing on these cryptographical puzzles for winning a reward, at least that is what it sounds like in theory. Now here comes the catch. When it comes to mining on a major network of the public blockchain, it needs a lot of power over a period. As the number of people investing in powerful and advanced hardware increases, thee power it requires increases as well. At the moment, all those who are making use of a low-powered setup are not likely to win. However, I still consider this to be a viable pastime for all the hobbyists and enthusiasts out there.

Selecting the mining hardware

Before you can get started with Ethereum mining, you will need a specific computer hardware that will be dedicated to working full-time on mining Ether. Two types of equipment are made use of for mining. These are CPUs and GPUs. GPUs have got a better hash rate; this means that they are better at guessing the answers to the puzzles and they can do so quickly as well. At present, GPUs are the only option that a miner would have.

The task of picking a GPU can be quite complex. A quick search on the Internet will provide you with different options regarding the ones that are better based on their hash rate, their power consumption, and also the initial expense incurred for procuring the card. You can build your mining rig or buy one of the ready-to-use ones that are available these days. By making use of a profitability calculator, you will get to know the amount of Ether tokens that you will be able to earn at the given harsh-rate of the hardware and whether this will be sufficient for covering the expenses incurred while helping you make a profit on the side.

Installation of the software

After you have managed to select the mining hardware, the next step would be the installation of the software necessary for mining. Before all this, if you want to be a miner, then you will need to install a client for connecting to the Ethereum network. Programmers who are familiar with the command line can go ahead and install Geth that runs on the Ethereum node written in "GO" (the scripting language), or any of the different clients. I downloaded Geth from the

Internet, and you can do the same too. Download the version that would suit your operating system (Windows, iOS, or even Linux). After you have downloaded it, you will need to unzip the file and run it. Once it has been successfully installed, your node will be able to connect with the other nodes and thereby connect with the Ethereum network. You not only can start mining Ether, but the Ethereum network will provide you with an interface for the deployment of your Smart Contracts and also for sending transactions by making use of the command line.

Testing

You can also mine "test" Ether on your network for experimenting with Smart Contracts or Dapps (activities that would need the use of tokens). You don't need any fancy hardware to mine on a test network. Your home computer will do, as long as you have installed Geth or any other client. However, mining fake Ether won't be lucrative for sure.

Installing Ethminer

If you want to mine "real" Ether, then you will need to install the Ether mining software. As I mentioned earlier, once you have got the necessary mining hardware and your node is connected to the Ethereum network, you will need to download Ethminer. Depending on the operating system you are using, you will need to download the appropriate version. Once you have done this, then your node will now be a part of the official Ethereum network. I found it difficult to mine Ether on my own. That's when I discovered that miners tend to pool together their computational resources for creating mining pools. These pools help in improving the chances of being able to solve the cryptographical puzzles and of earning Ether. Whenever a profit is made, then the same would be divided amongst the members of the pool according to a pre-decided ratio or the amount of power that was contributed by each of the miners. There are different factors that you are involved in this process, and a mining pool can be quite temporary. The computational power of a pool will keep on changing, and different factors will help you in deciding the pool you want to join. The payout structure for mining pools will be different. Some mining pools might have a signup process so that the miners will be able to connect to the pool and start mining Ether.

The mining world is quite dynamic. If you want to get into mining, then you will need to gather the necessary equipment and get started.

Conclusion

I want to thank you once again for purchasing this book.

Investing in Ethereum is a good idea, and you will have realized this by now. All the information that has been provided in this book will help you in making an informed investment. Once you are aware of how it functions, its benefits, the method in which it is traded, and the process of getting started, all that is left for you to would be to get started.

Ethereum is the future of investments, and it is here to stay. It overcomes all the disadvantages that fiat money poses. Learning about Ethereum will help you in making the most of your investments and help you make better financial choices as well.

Thank you and all the best!

Bibliography

What Is Ethereum and How to Make Money With Ethereum?

By Alex Y

https://managingyourfinance.com/what-is-ethereum-and-how-to-make-money-with-ethereum

How Do I Buy Ethereum?

By Nathan Reiff | July 6, 2017 — 11:32 AM EDT

http://www.investopedia.com/news/how-do-i-buy-ethereum/?lgl=rira-baseline-vertical

Top 10 Amazing Facts About Ethereum

July 13, 2017 Mina

http://www.meaningfulwomen.com/top-10-amazing-facts-about-ethereum/

What is Ethereum?

By Chris Jagers | Updated July 13, 2017 — 1:30 PM EDT

http://www.investopedia.com/articles/investing/022516/what-ethereum.asp

Who Created Ethereum?

Authored by Alyssa Hertig

http://www.coindesk.com/information/who-created-ethereum/

What is Ether?

Alyssa Hertig

http://www.coindesk.com/information/what-is-ether-ethereum-cryptocurrency/

Beginner's Guide to Ethereum Mining in 2017 – How to Mine Ethereum on Your PC?

BY STEVEN HAY ON JULY 11, 2017 - UPDATED ON JULY 19TH, 2017

https://99bitcoins.com/guide-ethereum-mining-how-to-mine-ethereum/

Ethereum Mining 101: Your Complete Guide

Ameer Rosic, ContributorCEO of Blockgeeks

03/01/2017 10:20 am ET

http://www.huffingtonpost.com/entry/ethereum-mining-101-your-complete-guide_us_58b6e1eee4b02f3f81e44e9f

How to buy Bitcoin in seconds from your smartphone

Todd Haselton | @robotodd

Saturday, 24 Jun 2017 | 9:46 AM ET

http://www.cnbc.com/2017/06/24/how-to-buy-bitcoin-ethereum.html